113 Crickets

113 Crickets—Tech meets Literature

113 Crickets *is a Silicon Valley-based literary journal published quarterly by Dymaxicon. Each issue of* 113 Crickets *contains a selection of prose, poetry, and short stories by new and established writers, alongside extracts from Dymaxicon's own literary publications.*

113 Crickets *embraces its Silicon Valley roots by especially seeking writers from the tech world, and featuring published authors and poets with connections to the Bay Area.*

©2012 by Dymaxicon
An imprint of Agile Learning Labs
Silicon Valley, USA

ISBN# 978-1-937965-06-8

copyediting by Rayna Arendain
layout and typography by Hillary Louise Johnson
cover design and photography by Tobias Mayer

113 Crickets

Summer 2012

*an anthology of poetry,
prose and short stories*

DYMAXICON

Contents

113 Crickets Summer 2012

Welcome, or welcome back, to *113 Crickets*. This is our second volume of work and we continue our quest to offer new, cutting edge work to delight and inspire the reader. The summer issue contains work by seven writers, new and established, working in a variety of literary styles.

Three of the writers are drawn from Dymaxicon's own pool of talent—Nancy Rommelmann, Walt Foreman and Ricki Grady. Nancy Rommelmann, a journalist, and Walt Foreman, a screenwriter, both have short fiction collections due to be published by Dymaxicon later this year— *Transportation* and *Beer in the Sun* respectively. This issue features two stories from each collection to whet your appetite for their upcoming books. We have included the introduction to Ricki Grady's *Bebop Garden*, a lighthearted and witty description of her improvisational approach to gardening, which was published by Dymaxicon in 2011. Ricki's improvisational approach to gardening in some ways mirrors emergent processes in software development, and our readers in the IT field may find inspiration in the gardening metaphor.

From the software world itself, we are pleased to present seven poems by Liz Keogh, a published poet and a well-respected Agile coach and facilitator. Liz Keogh's poems are preceded by an interview-style dialog with *113 Crickets* where she talks about the connections between poetry and computer code creation.

Two other writers in this issue are Mark Eagleton,

a previously unpublished writer from Queensland, Australia, whose collection of vignettes painfully reveal the residue of sadness people may live with following a tragedy, and Cindy Lee Berryhill, a *Rolling Stone*-commended singer/songwriter and recording artist based in Southern California, whose poetry has a lyrical quality congruent with her musical compositions.

Closing off the volume is a collection of ten poems by James Franco, inspired by the music of The Smiths. Actor/writer/director James Franco was born and raised in Palo Alto, in the heart of Silicon Valley and the poems are inspired by his experiences as a teenager living in this area.

We hope you enjoy this volume. We look forward to reading your reviews, or hearing from you directly if you are interested in contributing work or supporting us through ad placement. You'll find us at *113crickets.com*, and you can follow us on Facebook and Twitter to receive up-to-date news of our progress towards the Autumn 2012 issue.

Tobias Mayer, editor

Nancy Rommelmann

Nancy Rommelmann was born in New York City, raised in Brooklyn, and did an 18-year stint in Los Angeles, where she became a long-form journalist. Her articles and profiles—about serial killers, literary hoaxers, dishonest cops, heiresses-turned-drunks and much manner in between—appear in LA Weekly, Los Angeles Times, The New York Times, Reason *and* Byliner.

Nancy's first novel, The Bad Mother *was published by Dymaxicon in 2011. Her memoir of growing up in 1970s Brooklyn Heights,* The Queens of Montague Street, *was digitally released on New Year's Day 2012, and excerpted in* The New York Times Magazine. *Her collection of short fiction,* Transportation—*from which the work presented here is extracted—will be published by Dymaxicon in October 2012.*

Nancy is currently based in Portland, where she reviews books for The Oregonian, *and is at work on* To The Bridge, *a book of nonfiction based on the story of Amanda Stott-Smith, who threw her two young children from a Portland bridge in 2009. More information and links to Nancy's work can be found at nancyrommelmann.com.*

Tom Moore

"He is not!" screamed Tom Moore. His nose was packed with watery mucus from trying not to cry.

"Is so," taunted Kenny Figa. "Your dad's a faggot who kisses other guys on the you-know-what." Kenny spit into the cement drainpipe Tom had climbed into.

Tom tried to concentrate so his teeth would stop chattering, he didn't want Kenny to hear them; he wanted to rush out of the pipe and knock him down. But he didn't make a run at flabby Kenny Figa with his orange hair, didn't run for home and tell his dad what happened. Tom wasn't supposed to break his father's concentration while he was writing.

"You don't know anything!" Tom screamed. He'd been riding his new bike around the cul-de-sac when Kenny came up the street. He'd stood there with his dough stomach showing between his shirt and shorts, asking for a turn every fifteen seconds. Tom didn't want Kenny's sweaty butt on his bike. When Kenny lunged, Tom skidded out, scrambling to keep hold of the handlebars as Kenny grabbed the bike and pulled. Then Kenny called his dad that, said it with such spite that Tom felt side-swiped and let go. He'd sat on the ground and watched Kenny's butt sag around the seat of his bike. He was trying to figure out a way to knock Kenny over when the fat boy rode straight at him, and Tom did a fast backward crawl into the pipe, which had been left at the top of the street by some construction crew, no one knew which one, there was so much building going on in the neighborhood.

Tom sat in the pipe and listened to Kenny ride the bike in circles and thought about his father. His father was into environmental stuff and responsibility, and after dinner two nights before had taken Tom to knock on people's doors and discuss the problem of the pipe. Tom noticed none of the neighbors seemed very interested, they listened to his father and nodded but didn't want to sign the petition his father had typed. He told Tom he wasn't discouraged; that sometimes "convincing people what's good for them is a thankless job." When they came to the Figas' house, one in a row of small houses close to the intersection, Tom asked his father not to knock.

"The Figas are part of this block, Tom, they'll want to be part of the solution," his father said, in that even tone that made things sound casual and serious at the same time.

"No." Tom grabbed his father's arm before he knew he was going to do it. His father stared at Tom's hand.

"What are you doing, Tom?"

Tom couldn't explain why he didn't want his father to knock, he just had a bad feeling. "They're probably not home," Tom said.

"One way to find out," his father said. Tom stayed on the sidewalk at the edge of the Figas' dead yard and watched his father knock. A big pale spot appeared behind the screen door—Mr. Figa's face.

"How are you, Mike?" Tom's father asked. Tom was amazed his father knew Mr. Figa's first name.

"Good. What's going on?" Mr. Figa pushed open the door and held it there with his hand. Tom noticed Mr. Figa's fingers were fat, and they all looked the same length. Tom also noticed Mr. Figa was wearing only a pair of shorts and slippers, and wondered if his father felt embarrassed, standing that close to Mr. Figa's naked stomach.

"Beer?" asked Mr. Figa.

"No thanks," said Tom's father. Neither he nor Tom's mother drank alcohol. "Listen, Mike, I don't know if you've noticed that pipe at the end of the street." Tom's father nodded in the direction of the pipe.

Mr. Figa came onto the stoop and looked up the hill.

"Well, you can't see it from here," said Tom's father. "It's at the end, near our house."

Mr. Figa made a snuffling sound, walked heavily down his stoop, and scuffed his slippers on the concrete walkway. Once he'd reached the sidewalk, and before squinting up the block in a serious way, he glanced down at his beer, up at Tom, and winked.

"We can go take a look," said Tom's father, walking up to Tom and Mr. Figa.

"That's okay, I know what a pipe looks like," said Mr. Figa. "What's the problem?"

"Well, I was wondering. Would you happen to know who left it there?"

Mr. Figa took a sip of beer. "Can't say as I do, Mr. Moore." Tom noticed Mr. Figa pronounced it Maw. "Maybe it was left over from that Jacuzzi they put behind your house."

Tom's father rubbed the bridge of his nose. "No, no, we made sure all refuse was properly carted off." Tom's father laughed in a fake way. "For what the contractor charged, they could have hauled it away twice!"

Mr. Figa nodded. "Yeah, they'll getcha every time." He looked toward his door. "Well, we'll see you later."

Tom's father touched Mr. Figa on the arm. Mr. Figa looked at the hand. "You need something, Mr. Moore?"

"I came up with two solutions," said Tom's father, moving his hand to the clipboard he was carrying. "The first would be, we designate someone on the block to call the city and find out who's responsible for hauling it off."

"You got my vote," said Mr. Figa.

"Yes... and I'm happy to do it. But, in the eventuality that the city says it's not their problem, I suggest we hire a hauling company to get rid of it."

Mr. Figa smacked his belly a few times. Tom noticed it didn't appear flabby but firm. "My brother-in-law's got a truck big enough," said Mr. Figa. "But it'll cost you."

"Great, great, if we need to have it hauled, we'll call him. As far as cost, I propose the people on the block split it. Create a block association kitty of sorts."

Mr. Figa pushed out his lower lip and looked into his can of beer.

"For when this sort of thing comes up," said Tom's father.

Mr. Figa squinted up the hill in a way that looked as though he were trying not to look at Tom's father.

"I'm sorry, Mike, am I stepping on toes here?"

Tom understood Mr. Figa didn't want to talk about it anymore. "Dad, you have to help me with that World War II report," Tom said.

Tom saw the interruption stretch his father's patience. "Can we talk about it in a few minutes, Son?"

"But it's important, Dad, and it has to be done by tomorrow."

Mr. Figa looked at Tom. "Kids. Always something, huh?" he said, smiling at Tom's father. Tom saw that something in Mr. Figa had uncoiled, and this uncoiling made Tom relax. He and his father could stay now, if they needed to.

"Yes, well," said Tom's father. He slapped the clipboard to his hip. "I'll be in touch, Mike. When I find out what's going on."

"You do that, Mr. Moore."

"I thought we finished your report last week," Tom's father said as they walked back up the hill. Tom knew it wouldn't be hard to make up something else he needed. He wished his father would stop rubbing him on the shoulder, he was sure Mr. Figa was watching them. He didn't get up the nerve to turn around and look until they rounded the bend, and by then it was too late.

Tom heard the bike's wheels slide and the bike drop. He saw Kenny's legs, heard him huff, saw him bend down and squint into the pipe. He was easily too big to crawl in.

"Faggot!" he screamed, banging his hand against the pipe and chanting an Indian drumbeat that Tom knew was incorrect: his fifth grade class had learned that the sound of the drum was not, "DUH-duh-duh-duh," like in cartoons, but the sound of a heartbeat, "duh-DUH,

duh-DUH."

"That's not how it goes," Tom said.

"You say something, sissy boy?" Kenny threw a handful of pebbles, one hit Tom in the mouth. He scooted back, into a puddle, wetting the seat of his pants.

"You're a sissy!" Tom screamed. His voice made an echo. "You are! You're a faggot sissy!" Tom's head started to buzz. "And you're fat and stupid, too!" Now Tom wanted to punch Kenny in the mouth repeatedly until he bled. He imagined grabbing Kenny's shirt and spitting in his face, or biting his nose, roaring until Kenny knew he'd been beaten.

"Did you hear what I said?" Tom shouted. The echo was loud and woofy. Sound waves. Tom knew they were how bats avoided careening into the walls of their caves.

"Whaaa!" Tom yelled, to hear his voice again. This time there was an empty quality to the yell, as if, once it left the pipe, there was nothing for the sound to bounce against. Tom tensed. "Hello? Anybody there?"

The stillness that came back told him Kenny was gone. Probably. Tom began inching out of the pipe feet first, pausing at the pipe's opening to see if Kenny was being quiet on purpose. But Kenny was gone.

"Whoo!" Tom yelled. He wanted to stand on the top of his street and shout, "You lost! I won!" Instead, he hopped on the pipe, stood with his arms up and his face to the sky, and pretend-shouted like the roar of a crowd. Then he took off running down the street. Halfway home, he realized he'd left his bike, and began slowly walking back, thinking that, in times of victory, things get left behind. His class had learned that people fleeing the Nazis had to abandon expensive art, and only now was some of it being found and reclaimed by its rightful owners. As Tom neared the cul-de-sac, he began to feel anxious, something bad was happening, he knew it before he saw his bike was gone.

Tom sat on his bed, whittling a stick of wood that came with the "Li'l Whittler" set he'd received the Christmas before. The wood was balsa, very soft, meant to be cut with a Teflon "safety whittler" Tom's father had expressed scorn for. Over the protests of Tom's mother he'd given Tom his old penknife, the one he'd used as a boy during summers at the family camp in Maine. Tom cut the pulpy wood to a sliver in four strokes before starting on another piece, not caring that shards were getting all over the carpet, wanting in fact to make a mess, or to cut his thumb. He made a few hard, careless strokes. The wood split and bent at a right angle. Tom threw the mess on the floor and lay on his bed, staring at the ceiling. At 6:35, there was a knock on the door.

"What?" he asked.

"We're ready for you to set the table. Whoa," said his father. "Looks like Paul Bunyon's been here."

Tom gave a dramatic sigh.

"You remember when I read that to you, Tom? Remember Babe the Blue Ox?"

Tom turned away from his father.

"What's wrong, son?"

"Nothing," said Tom. He was making his voice sound angry on purpose.

"Okay," said his father, rolling a big splinter between his

fingers, letting the wood-dust float to the floor. "Better perk it up then, dinner's in ten."

Tom stared at the wall, at a thirty-year old photo of his father and Gampy Moore. Gampy Moore had been a lawyer to President Lyndon Johnson and a lot of other people in the government, all Tom's male relatives had been lawyers, back to the 1700s. Tom's father was ten in the picture, and looked just like Tom, except he was wearing a coat and tie. Gampy Moore was wearing a jacket, too, and had a tired, or mad, or impatient look around his eyes, as though he had a lot of places to be rather than posing for a picture on the lawn with the fifth of his seven children. Tom got off the bed to straighten the photo. It fell off the wall.

"Here," said his father, coming around the bed and helping Tom find the nail, which was bent. His father pushed the nail in the hole and re-hung the picture, which fell again immediately, something that made Tom irrationally angry.

Tom's father picked up the picture and held it. "We'll take care of it later."

"I can do it," Tom said, finding the nail and trying to unbend it.

"Tom, don't worry about it. Manuel is coming to look at the deck tomorrow, I'll ask him to put in another nail."

"But I can do it," Tom said, wrestling the nail, feeling himself start to sweat. His father laid his hand on top of Tom's.

"Son, relax."

Tom pulled his hand away and fell back on the bed. He pinched the nail between his fingers and stared at it. "He called you a faggot."

"What? Who called me that?"

Tom set his jaw. "Kenny Figa. He called you a faggot."

Both Tom's parents were writers, and had taught him that there were no bad words, only strings of letters. But still.

"Tom, you know I'm not a homosexual. I'm with Mommy."

"Who's with me?" Tom's mother came from the hall, holding a limp bunch of basil.

"It's nothing," said his father, opening his arm to his mother's perfect roundness, admitting the warm beige cashmere of her.

Tom stopped musing on how his parents fit together, he didn't want to see happy pretty things. "Doesn't it bother you that he called you a faggot?"

Tom's father looked at Tom's mother. "No, Son, it doesn't," he said.

Tom sat up on the bed. "You're saying it really doesn't matter to you?" He didn't like how squeaky his voice was getting. "How can you say that? I don't believe you!"

"What I'm saying is, it doesn't matter because it isn't true, Tom." His father was calm, very calm. "And if it doesn't bother me, it shouldn't bother you."

Tom flung himself back on the bed and put his pillow over his face. Someone tugged at the pillow; Tom heard his parents saying, "Tom... Tom," in a way that sounded as though they were laughing. Tom pulled off the pillow and clutched it to his stomach. His mother rubbed his hair off his high forehead.

"Tommy, if you let every little thing everyone ever

thought to say bother you, you'd have no time to do any-thing else." She smiled her high-wattage smile at Tom, at her husband. "I'm going to make the pesto now. Help me, Johnny?"

Tom's father stood. "When you're ready, come set the table," he said.

Tom went and sat in his closet. Leaning against one wall, he looked at stuff that had meant something to him: the elaborate train set, a gift from Gampy Moore that had held sway in the living-room for two years; the Paris ver-sion of Monopoly, which they'd purchased during what his parents called a "writing sojourn" in France; the tele-scope; the series of costumes leftover from various pag-eants at school. He rested his elbows on his bent knees and stared at the little plastic glow-in-the-dark pump-kins and witches and cats he and his mother had af-fixed to one wall on Halloween three years earlier, when Tom had a cold and couldn't go trick-or-treating. He'd put on his Power Ranger costume anyway, and by flash-light he and his mother had made his closet a haunted house, while she told the story about the time her candy bag had been snatched by a group of kids not from her neighborhood, and how the next day her father had tak-en her to the Whitman store and bought her the largest Sampler they had. "And it turned out to be the Halloween I remember most fondly," she'd said, pressing on a little ghost, the flashlight beam lighting her eyelashes from beneath and firing through her blonde hair. Even wear-ing the black witch's hat she wore every Halloween, Tom thought she was the most beautiful and the nicest mom-my in the world. Tom reached out and picked at the little ghost, which came off the wall attached to a quarter-sized chip of paint. Tom fit the whole thing back in place, balancing the chip in the hole it had left.

Tom didn't say anything about the bike for four days, until his father asked if he wanted to go for a ride.

"I can't," Tom said. "I don't have the bike anymore."

They were in the garage, standing by the boxes of heirloom encyclopedias his father said demanded their own bookshelf, but which in the meantime sat warping from exposure.

"What do you mean, you don't have it anymore?"

"I lost it," Tom said, toeing his sneaker against the cement floor.

"When did you lose it?" His father tapped his reflective bike helmet against his thigh. "How do you lose a bike?"

"I don't want to talk about it," said Tom, wanting to go upstairs, to sit in his closet.

"Whoa, ho, hold on," his father said. "Come here."

Tom came and stood before his father. Tom saw a light sheen on his father's forehead, a high forehead Tom's mother called "patrician." Tom wasn't sure what that meant, something about looking like one's forebears.

"I'm not mad, Tom, I just want you to explain to me what happened."

Tom wanted to say it was his father's fault the bike was gone; that if Kenny Figa hadn't called him a faggot, none of this would have happened; Tom and his father could have taken a ride like they did every Saturday, they could have ridden downtown and shared a secret café mocha. (Tom's mother forbid Tom to have caffeine.) Everything was ruined.

"I lost it the other day," Tom said, looking at the floor. "I was riding up at the top of the street and I saw that pipe and I thought it would be cool to explore it, so I went inside—"

"You went in that pipe?" His father's voice squeaked up, which Tom knew meant he was trying to hold in his temper; Tom's father thought losing one's temper was "barbaric." "Tom, listen, there could be rats in that pipe, or brown spiders, you could have gotten trapped." His father put on his helmet. "You have to use your head, son."

"Sorry," Tom mumbled.

"I'm just concerned for your safety, you know that."

"I know."

Tom watched his father secure his jeans-cuff so it wouldn't get caught in the bike chain. His father had a thing about safety. "I'm going for a ride. Tell your mother I'll be back in time for lunch. She's made that soup we like so much. Yum-yum."

Tom didn't ask if his father meant beef-noodle or leek because he didn't care, he didn't feel he could swallow even a sip of water. He watched his father ride down the hill on his high-performance bike. Tom's was a copy in miniature, something his father had special-ordered. Yet there'd been no punishment for its disappearance, as if bikes did that on their own sometimes, they evaporated, and when they did one simply bought a new one.

As soon as his father was out of sight, Tom ran down the hill. He saw his father stop at the intersection, look both ways, and signal before crossing traffic. Tom slowed to a walk as he reached the Figas'. Mr. Figa was in the driveway, washing his car. Tom watched him dunk a rag into gray bucket water.

"Hey there," Mr. Figa said, slopping the rag on the hood of the car. "Just saw your old man ride by."

Tom nodded. "Yes, sir."

"He's one of those exercise freaks," Mr. Figa said, winking at Tom.

"I guess so." Tom was aware that he was standing unnaturally still.

Mr. Figa bent slowly over the hood, keeping his eyes on Tom. "Looking for something, kid?"

"Yes, sir. My bike."

Mr. Figa squeezed the rag onto the dirt alley that ran along driveway. "Bike? What's it look like?"

Tom was about to explain that it was a copy of his father's, navy with a red racing stripe, an 18-speed hybrid. "Ask Kenny," he said.

"Can't do that, he's off at Pop Warner," said Mr. Figa. "You know what that is?"

"No."

"It's like Little League, for football. You know what Little League is, don't you?"

Tom had played Little League for two years, but hadn't liked it much. "I did Little League for two years, but I didn't like it much."

"Oh, no? How come?"

"Well, all the parents would get overexcited, pretending they didn't care if you won, but really they did. Plus, it was always hot. I just didn't like it. I'm doing swimming now instead."

"Oh, yeah? You swimming over at the Y?"

"No, my mom drives me twice a week after school to the college."

"Yeah? That's good," Mr. Figa said, putting down the rag and picking up a bottle of beer. "That's a nice mom, that'll do that for ya."

"Yes, sir."

"So, your mom doesn't work?"

"Well, she works at home. She's a writer."

"Yeah? What does she write?"

"Plays and stuff. She writes a lot of journals, too."

"She get paid a lot for that?"

Tom had no idea whether his mother got paid. It seemed as if Mr. Figa were trying to trick him into saying something that would make his mother look bad. "I don't know. But even if I did I wouldn't tell you."

Mr. Figa nodded. "Tell you what, kid. Hey, what's your name anyway?"

"Tom. Tom Moore."

"Tell you what, Tom Moore, when Kenny gets back, I'll send him up to your house and you can ask him about your bike."

"Okay. I guess," Tom said, stubbing his sneaker on the sidewalk. He noticed the Figas lawn was all dust, and that there were tire marks in it. "I know Kenny took my bike, Mr. Figa."

Mr. Figa held his beer in front of his large stomach. "Yeah? You sure about that?"

"I'm sure."

"How come your father didn't say nothing to me about it?"

"I didn't tell my father."

Mr. Figa considered Tom. "That's not his thing, stolen bikes? More a leftover pipe kind of guy?"

"I guess so."

"You know, when we was kids growing up, a leftover pipe on the street would've been a treasure. Would've kept us busy for months."

Tom didn't know what to say to that.

"You know, space-ship, club-house, place to do things you didn't want your folks to see, like smoke a cigarette."

Mr. Figa seemed to be waiting for Tom to say something. "Uh huh," said Tom.

"You smoke, Tom Moore?"

Tom had turned ten two months earlier, and thought that maybe this was another trick question. His mother said cigarettes were 'abhorrent,' which is what she called things she really hated, though Tom sometimes saw his father sneak one, at night, up on the second tier of their garden. "Not yet, sir."

"Good. Don't start. Nasty habit. Plus, it'll kill ya."

"Yes, sir."

"Lung cancer, terrible way to go. Months if not years writhing in pain, spitting up black blood clots."

"Yes, sir."

"You ever drink a beer?"

"No, sir. My parents don't drink."

"That makes sense," Mr. Figa said, running his thumb over the mouth of his beer bottle. "Want a sip?"

Tom didn't really want a sip, but he didn't not want a sip. "Sure."

Mr. Figa handed him the beer. The brown glass was cold, with beads of water on the outside.

"Right here?" Tom asked, looking toward his house.

"You don't have to," said Mr. Figa, though he didn't hold out his hand to take back the beer.

Tom read the bottle: Michelob. He took a sip. It tasted sort of like liquid bread, sour but also refreshing. Tom closed his eyes and took another sip.

"Okay, that'll do ya," said Mr. Figa, taking his beer. "Go around the back of that shed back there."

Tom wiped his mouth with his hand, and looked down the drive, at a small storage shed. "Go behind there?"

"That's what I said."

Tom walked around the side of the car where Mr. Figa wasn't. Tom was afraid Mr. Figa might follow him behind the shed, or that Kenny was hiding there, listening to everything that they'd said, waiting to pound him. Tom stopped halfway down the drive to look at Mr. Figa, who was looking at him, holding the red rag in his fat fist.

"Go on, Tom Moore," Mr. Figa said.

Tom walked around to the back of the shed. There was nothing there but a rusted lawn mower. Tom started to get scared. Maybe Mr. Figa was going to come back here and do something to him, Tom's parents had had a serious discussion with him about not talking to strangers and now he was in the Figas back yard. Not that the Figas were really strangers, they lived on the same block and everything, but still, he'd never seen his parents talk to the Figas. Except the other night. Tom looked at the warped chain-link fence marking off the Figas yard from a small yard like it. His heart was pounding in his ears, and his throat felt as if it were closing. Should he try to go over the fence? Or should he walk back past Mr. Figa?

He peered around the shed to see how far it was to the sidewalk, and saw his bike, lying on its side in the yard, its front wheel resting against a cracked-up baby-pool. Tom picked up the bike. It looked fine. His shirt was sticking to his back. He tried to walk the bike at a normal speed back down the driveway.

"Thank you, Mr. Figa," Tom said.

"No problem. Better get yourself a lock for that thing."

"Yes, sir."

"Can't always trust that daddy's gonna be there to look out for you. Gotta look out for yourself, right?"

"Yes, sir."

"All right then, get outta here," said Mr. Figa, going back to his car.

Tom rolled the bike into the street and got on. Maybe he'd take a ride into town. His parents didn't mind him riding by himself, they said they trusted him, it was just the intersection they were afraid of. He should probably go home first, tell his mom he was leaving, but downtown was only five blocks away, he wouldn't be gone very long. Tom got excited as he pushed off, thinking he might run into his father, and how surprised he'd be.

Maybe You Can Save Me

I saw you the instant I came through the door, Mary, I meant to find you and there you were, alone and radiant amid the artificial light and the music, I watched you from the doorway, and thought, I can go over there and sit quietly and she will understand, Mary, won't that be something, to sit quietly while everyone shouts and sways and the girls throw back their heads and show their throats, they're here to have a good time, I shouldn't deny them that, Mary, we can dance, too, if you'd like, after all they're playing the real thing, the real swing, you don't hear it as much as before, now it's more moonlight stuff, the Flamingos, I like them, I do, but I suspect I'm sentimental, I have a soft spot for Dorsey and those boys, if you know what I mean, Mary, if you'd like to dance I'm happy to, though I can only see you from the waist up, such a tiny waist tapering below the tablecloth, you look as though you'd be light on your feet, but I'm being coy, Mary, I've seen you dance, it was four nights ago, I saw you here, you were dancing with a big yellow-haired fellow, his arm looked like a leg of lamb against your small

back, the silk of your dress, you were wearing a dress like
the one you have on now only it wasn't coral-colored but
jade, I can see it's real silk, did you know we couldn't get
silk here for years, Mary, your hair, too, looks like silk,
like black mercury, I imagine it would slip through my
fingers, not that I'm going to do that, no, I'm not going to
touch your hair, I mean, not now, no, Mary, I'd never let
you slip, if that's what you thought I was saying, safe-
guarding you means a great deal to me, and yet the way
you sit here, all alone, your friend off in the powder room,
you barely look as though you need my protection, up
close your face is inscrutable, I can't tell if you're looking
at me, Mary, can you hear me above the noise, I'm saying
you don't appear fragile, you look as though you have a
protective skin, like that of an almond, something cru-
cial and inseparable, Mary, I'd like to make it plain I understand, I think it's right and necessary that you protect
yourself, and if you don't mind my saying so, I think your
people had to develop resistance, had to endure so very
much, the way it all ended and the devastation, it's a tragedy, a tragedy of cataclysmic proportions, I don't care
what shore you're on, it's not to be celebrated for any reason, yes, I admit, when it was over and I went to the pa-
rade I felt, I think many of us felt, swept up on a wave of
relief and euphoria that I've never quite stopped feeling,
except the relief part, and the euphoria, you wouldn't expect as much, but the responsibility is exhausting, it's
hard to get real rest, and I suppose I sound weak but I
keep wondering if there's a cure for it, Mary, when I saw
you the other night, so serene, so secure, accepting the
hands of men but not laughing with your mouth open

like other girls, I began to get the idea that you might have some insight into a cure, that's expressly why I came here tonight, why I walked over to you with my coat and hat still wet from the snow, while my buddy, my friend, fetched the drinks, drinks for all of us, he and I can sit with you and your friend when she gets back from powdering her face, that's how you keep your skin so white and smooth, bet you didn't know I knew about rice paper and powder, but I went over there, Okinawa, yes, but I did come home early, I had to, no crime in that, no crime, boy, it's loud in here, and hot, I'll take off my coat, I'll hang it over this chair, out of your way, Mary, if you will turn your face to me, if you pivot your face one inch in my direction, then I'll tell you about something I saw this afternoon that really impressed me, it did, I saw this woman walking a pack of dogs, must have been twelve little dogs, a dozen yapping little dogs on leashes in front of her, she was a good looking girl, she wore a tweed suit and one of those little tam hats, she wasn't beautiful like you, Mary, of course not, but a good looking girl, a girl your family might have known, a girl who might have lived on your block, that kind of girl, with smooth brown hair cut to her chin, a boy might have had a crush on a girl like that, his parents might have liked her a lot and even encouraged marriage or something but that stuff, what is that, that happens in the movies, anyway, I didn't know this girl, I'm just explaining what type she was, she was a familiar type, but what she was doing that impressed me was, she was in control of these dogs, in complete control, she'd give their leashes short tugs and the dogs would stop fussing or running or whatever it was the girl wanted them to do, it was pretty amazing, fairly amazing, though it could have been the types of dogs they were, terrier types with little bows at the front of their heads, and a few poodles, I think, though I'm not sure, I can't remember if there were poodles, I've heard poodles are mean, Mary, I'm going to sit down now, right here, look at all these people, I used to come here years ago, I'm certain I used to come here, this place has been popular forever, you probably didn't know that, having come from overseas only recently, how long have you been here, did I hear your friend say two years, Mary, she's been gone a while, hasn't she, maybe on her way back she met a fella, maybe she's dancing, maybe she's dancing with my friend right now, maybe I should see about getting us some drinks, Mary, I see you have a drink already, but a fresh one would be good, something cool, I could use the ice, it would be a good idea to put a piece of ice on the back of my neck, it's hot in here, there's not much air, if I stand up maybe I can see if my friend is coming with the icy drinks, Mary, I didn't remember until just now that there's a balcony behind us, just a few feet behind us, if you turn your head a little you can see it, Mary, if you just turn your head, boy, it sure looks cool out there, look at the moonlight, so blue and shimmering off the water like that, oh heck, I sound like a song, and I'm not trying to, honestly, I'm not trying to be romantic or anything, Mary, perhaps I'll stroll out there, I imagine there are couples out there, staring over the lake, there's always a lake, they build these places on lakes in order to entice you into forgetting, Mary, from the back, with your cigarette poised, you look like a movie star, you look like Tokyo Rose, not that I ever met her, I saw a photo of her, the same one everyone saw, talking into a radio microphone, it looked like a posed photo to me, I'm not saying you look like her in the face, she wasn't young like you, Mary, people said terrible things about her and I can understand their feeling that way but I don't feel that way, she had to do what she had to do, just like we had to do what we had to do, we all had to, we're all human beings, and I think it's hard to know right from wrong in certain situations, in extreme situations, and who decides what is extreme when everyone is shouting and afraid, fear so thick it feels as though they're asking you to march through oil, and you have to do it, and most guys do it, most guys do, Rose, I mean Mary, I'm going to sit down again, I'm feeling better, what kind of guy needs moonlight when he can sit next to a beautiful girl such as yourself, let me light that for you, here Mary, there, Mary, you are so composed, you have this unreadable expression, Mary, this might sound like an oddball question, 'Boy, this guy's an oddball,' but what I want to ask is, you appear to have the ability to focus in or pull away, like a telescope, depending on the safety of the situation, is that right, the safety part, Mary, it's safe in here, isn't it, that's what I thought when I walked in, when I saw you and your friend sitting here, as I said, it's not the first time I've seen you, I saw you four nights ago, Mary, it sounds crazy but I haven't been able to stop thinking of you, the way you sit so still, I haven't stopped thinking about the way you sit, Mary, I was wondering how you do it, is it a cultural thing or are you somehow more secure after what's happened, which doesn't make sense, you should be the one not finding your footing, but here you are calm as a statue, and here I am sweating through my collar, Mary, oh Mary, if you would turn your face and look at me, if my face could fill your frame for a moment I might calm down, settle down, whew, okay, Mary, it's cold, I'm cold all of a sudden, perhaps I'll put my coat back on, put on that coat and hey, Mary, you know what I'd like to do, I'd like to go out in the snow and take a walk, and I would like to take you with me, I could hold your hand and keep you warm while we take a walk across a long snowy field, maybe you've never done that, I could show you that, there's no reason not to, except that we're here and maybe we should be dancing, I'll dance if you want to, only I don't feel quite up to it, even though I came here with that in mind, with you in mind, with the idea of holding you in my arms in mind, and yet getting on the floor, with all those people, look at them, they all look as though they're enjoying themselves, do you think that's possible, what are the odds of four hundred people being happy in the same place at the same time, a needle in a haystack, is what it is, Mary, that's an expression, meaning the thing is hard if not impossible to find, the needle being so little and a haystack so big, but you probably know that phrase already, you probably know a lot of things I've been telling you, Mary, we can go onto the balcony and see the moonlight, that might be the thing to do, though I expect it's the same moonlight as over there, the moonlight you saw as a girl, before the trouble started and ended, before the decision about who to hate was taken out of a person's hands, one minute it was ours and the next we were handed pictures, it's simple, they told us, 'Hate them,' and for a lot of people I suspect hatred is as easy as turning on and off a faucet, don't ask questions, 'Loose lips sink ships' and you know, Mary, I think I see my friend coming with the drinks, is that him, if that's him we can say everything is swell, he'll come over and everything will be swell, everything will be normal, I'll hold my coat and there will be plenty of room for everything to be normal, routine's the thing, that's what they tell me, get out of the house, son, get some air, be with people your age, Mary, if you look around do these people look young, I can't really tell if they're young or they're people, that probably sounds queer, I've noticed that when a thing sounds truthful to me others react queerly, I'm trying to watch that, Mary, I hope you won't object to my being serious for one more minute, I know you have seen serious things, it seems impossible to me that you haven't seen serious things, and yet you're here, you're safe, and I'm here, and now we're supposed to dance, and what I'm saying is it doesn't quite fit, you can't make things right and make them fit after only two years and maybe you never can, but judging from the way everyone looks so bright and gay, they've moved on, they appear to understand it's time to dance, Mary, I'm asking if you understand it, your expression doesn't tell me, Mary, can you hear me, earlier tonight I told myself there was no reason to shout above the music, that I was going to sit and relax and I mean to, I'm going to enjoy myself because tonight it will be possible to do that, I'm going to see that dance floor and those gay young people and everything for what it is, it's victory, it's the continuation of humanity, I am going to sit here and recognize that and not be distracted by my spine being crushed into the metal chair or my hands, whew, hands are hot, Mary, may I hold your drink until mine comes, to cool down my paws, I'll just take it for a minute if I may, may I, it's okay, I'll just, oh Mary, if you would look at me, if you would smile at me, if your face changed expression at all, for me, I might move towards you, I might take you on that dance floor and hold you and bury my face in your hair, wet your hair with my breath and close my eyes and go down into that blackness and tell you I know, Mary, I know it's not manly to say these things, Mary, if you would turn your body toward me you might be my shield, that might change everything, Mary, you might whisper something in my ear that I've never thought before, a few words might clear away the fog, the idea of this makes me want to laugh, Mary, I'm afraid to laugh, afraid it might fill this room and drown the music and cause everyone to rush out, it would be a terrible stampede, people wouldn't know whether an angry god or some power beyond their control was forcing atonement on them, yes, I suppose this might be another idea of mine, Mary, perhaps not responding is your way of telling me there are a million alternatives for a young man, that's right, isn't it, and my alternative might be to get up, to go out onto the balcony and climb down the railing and take a walk along the lake, a walk through the snow in the moonlight, it sounds agreeable, it's a good choice, of course I'll go alone, Mary, I won't be taking your hand, what was that but an idea, a gesture, circling your small hand in mine, I'd thought of it as a steadying presence, but it's clear there's no reason to put that pressure on you, funny how things become clear so quickly, the new thing is before your eyes and you know it's your only choice, Mary, look at the crush of people at the door, laughing and excited to be here, without visible care, I see now it's silly of me, cruel, to deny them the music and lights, the faculty to walk through a door and forget, if circumstances were different I would surely take it, Mary, excuse me.

Liz Keogh

Liz Keogh is our featured software writer in this issue of 113 Crickets. *Liz studied Electronic and Electrical Engineering at the University of Bath in the UK, and went on to spend many years working as a software developer. During this time she was able to explore the emerging practices of Extreme Programming (XP) and Agile Software Development, both of which challenge the command and control approach to software development, and nurture the creativity of those engaged in the work. Liz is currently based in London and works as an independent coach and trainer, carrying forth the ideas formed in her early career.*

Liz has been studying and writing poetry from a young age and her work has appeared in Star*Line, Dreams and Nightmares, *the* Fortean Bureau *and* Mobius Poetry Magazine. *She is also a well-known international speaker on the Agile and IT conference circuit, and occasionally runs a haiku workshop at such events, exploring the parallels between poetry and code writing, and helping software development teams and individuals to use their intuition effectively. Liz is currently working on a fantasy novel, her first foray into long-form fiction.*

Interview with Liz Keogh

113 Crickets' *editor, Tobias Mayer spent time talking with Liz Keogh about her work as a software developer and poet, and how she combines the two—apparently disparate—fields of study.*

Tobias: Liz, you are well known in the software development world for your work as a coder, a coach and especially for your unique haiku workshops that you've now offered at many conferences. What is less known is that you are also a published poet. I'd like to start by asking about where you learned to write poetry.

Liz: I was taught to write poetry at school as part of my English Language GCSE. I think I was already becoming a goth at that stage. Goths can write really bad poetry without trying very hard. My friends and I also used to write poetry back and forth. I used to ask them for three random topics and turn them into a rhyming poem which related all three. I've always enjoyed playing with words.

Tobias: Please say a little more about how you identify as a goth, and what that means to you in terms of your life view, and your work.

Liz: For me, being a goth is about a focus on mortality. That might sound a bit morbid—goths are, aren't we?—but I find it quite positive and motivating. I've got a limited time left on this earth. Rather than getting depressed and mopey like the stereotype, a lot of us try to party, have fun and make a difference with our lives. There's still a lot of black and skull motifs going on, but having an awareness of death doesn't have to mean being miserable.

Tobias: What—or who—influences or inspires your writing?

Liz: The online Scifaiku group led me to look at haiku as a way of creating poetry, which helped me to use fewer metaphors and similes and to write in a more direct and descriptive style. I took Greek and Latin GCSE when I was young, and my mother's side of the family encouraged me to learn about classical mythology, so that influences my work quite strongly too—lots of poems about mythical creatures of various sorts. Neil Gaiman, Guy Gavriel Kay and Stephen King are some of my favorite writers. Neil Gaiman also has the classical influence; Guy Gavriel Kay's work reads like poetry anyway, and I love the way that some of Stephen King's looser writing—American slang, half-formed sentences written the way people would speak—causes dissonance within me. That's fun. *Bag of Bones* was one of my favorites, and seriously scary. I like horror films as well as books, and the way the tension leaves you feeling uncomfortable. My favorite poems do that too. I'm influenced more by individual poems than by poets, and I don't really want to dissect them here in case it kills them.

Tobias: Let's talk about your other recent passion: Behavior-driven development, or BDD as it's commonly known. Please begin by describing BDD, in layman's terms if you would, for our non-technical readers.

Liz: Using BDD, business experts, developers and testers are encouraged to talk through the various behaviors the end users may engage in with our system—each different context generating different results. It helps business people to clarify what they are asking for, testers to spot the scenarios that may be overlooked, and developers to understand more precisely what they should code. Talking through these examples of the user's engagement helps us spot where the desired behavior is unclear. Traditionally, software development methods have assumed that you could always define everything up-front. Nowadays we tend to work from the assumption that this isn't the case, and BDD helps with that.

Tobias: Does the story-telling aspect of BDD mesh with your poetry mindset at all? What are the connections for you?

Liz: In haiku, there's something we call the "haiku moment." That's the point at which our brain takes the two parts of the haiku and resolves the discrepancy between them, and that allows us to experience the haiku more directly. Similarly, when we're given a problem as developers—or even half a problem!—we already find ourselves experiencing the solution. That's given me a great deal of insight into the differences between that intuitive, problem-solving mindset and the problem-finding mindset necessary to really explore scenarios and find the missing ones and the places where uncertainty still exists. Everyone can interpret a haiku differently, and everyone gets a different experience from talking through scenarios.

Software development needs to be more like a renga—a

back-and-forth of small scenarios to explore the space, where the end result might not resemble the scenarios we began with, but will none the less be beautiful. I teach the haiku workshop so that participants can experience and recognize those moments of intuition and use them appropriately.

Tobias: I've always thought of code writing as a form of poetry. It's all about form and rhythm; often it's just as important what you leave out as what you put in, and the refactoring aspect of coding is very similar to editing. Do you see poetry in general—not just haiku—as being a useful study for those writing code? What improvements to quality do you think could be achieved if all coders considered themselves "software poets"?

Liz: I think every line of poetry should be surprising and interesting, and so should every line of code. When we write about sunlight, people remember warmth and summer days, early mornings and the smell of coffee. When developers read my code, I want them to remember the other projects they've worked on and imagine how this one is going to go forward. I can write about dark caves, and my readers might think of the stories of monsters they heard about as a child, or the feel of damp rock; there's wonder in poetry. I want other developers to see the name of a class or a method and not only understand it, but wonder how it works. Reading code should be a revelation, not a chore.

Tobias: I know you are working on your first novel at the moment. What are your other plans for the next year or two?

Liz: I've just come out of a development role and I've got a fair few speaking engagements this year, so I'm looking for part-time coaching to fit around that. Next year, who knows? I'm hoping to get south of the equator at some point—possibly visit Brazil, I've wanted to visit some developers there for such a long time. I'm signed up to go back to the USA in April, so planning for another year of traveling, visiting friends, and maybe even finishing the novel too.

Tobias: Thanks Liz. We're happy to be publishing a small set of your poems in this edition of 113 Crickets. *One of my hopes for this journal is that it will encourage the innate creativity I believe dwells in all software professionals. Your work in this area, and your involvement in this journal are important steps towards raising the collective creative consciousness of the IT industry.*

Blame Culture

screens denounce the trains
which turn up, sobbing,
in different shades of broken
we are berry-pressed
shoving our rib-cages out
so that we'll have room
when the doors scream
to breathe a second time

in the office, the usual list
the ones who died yesterday
whose man-months were enumerated
tallied, reassigned
during rush hour

the ones who came, rusted,
to the office of cohesion
crying for the drugs
that would make them work

the ones who grinned
mindlessly, nodded,
did whatever they were told
until you made them stop
glyph-ridden, just waiting
for their last letter

here, beneath the tubing
we breathe, clasp the scent
of our colleagues,
plunge our hands in
and hope that today
will be someone else's fault.

Earth: A Drinking Game

we sit in aluminium glow
shining from every surface
of the unwashed bar
grinning madly, full of teeth
little goblets in hand
playing the game;

every time the human mentions Earth
we down them with a flourish
slam them on the table
high-speed
wait for him to finish

conversation ranges from
the edges of religion
already well established
through politics—the humdrum
business of the day
psychic and psychological
tracked as easily
as the wet fingertips through
beer on the tabletop
over language, mathematics
the more we drink
the more we know we love
these nights; these hours of darkness
where only the bar rules
mark the minutes passing

"On Earth," he starts
and laughing, we lift glass
buy him another

"On Earth," accepting it
with a nod of gratitude
as if sarcasm and irony
weren't invented by them

"On Earth," he says,
"when we drank, ate bread
it made us brothers
and friends
with those who shared."

guilt is a new thing,
not easily digested;
our eyes fix, misty,
at the bottom of our glasses
we swallow the dregs
remembering why
we started this game in the first place.

At the Zoo

In this cage, ladies and gentlemen,
we have an Olympian Eagle;
the only one of his kind.
Notice the sharp beak, evolved
to tear at godflesh;
the talons, hard and muscled
for purchase on sweat-slicked granite.

He is not, despite his uniqueness
an endangered species.
This eagle will not die
until fire is returned to Olympus
and all human works lie shattered.
Over millennia, he's acquired a taste
for immortality.
Notice the sheen on his feathers,
the slow breath,
the way he looks past the bars
as if they were temporary.

Notice his eyes. He sees
only one target, only one prey,
created as he was to feed
on a single specimen;
a true monophage.
Even so, young man,
keep your hand out of the cage.
You are a most precious creation,
and you remind him
of his last meal.

The Sphinx Hypothesis

Sphinx riddles
observing through
ancient, myopic eyes
resolving quantum physics
in the dust storm
kicking up a fuss
over string theory
rediscovering gravity
with every heavy step

all the old questions
are long since answered;
no one wonders
at the three ages of man
yet still she devours
the best of the world
entrapping youth
into grey-haired wonder

the earth turns inexplicably
drawn to the sun
the desert pants and shifts
under her weight,
exposing the scorpid backs
of integral dunes
that solve and scatter

slaughtering mysteries
with every new equation
seeking blood to flinch
from dark matter in her sockets
and the tumbling, empty sky

she twists her tail
through polynomials
knotting foreheads
with old, mottled breath

stars pulse out code
in the wrinkled creases
of her smile

she laughs, spiral-toothed,
offering another riddle

seeking another answer.

Origins

they made your form
from memories of youth
and jealous sags of flesh

they made your mind
from stitched-up dreams
and interrogate cries

shambled into life
a roughly-crafted,
hurried thing:

don't hate them too much
there's no manual
on how to raise a child.

First published in Star*Line, *2005*

She married the wind

She married the wind on a Tuesday.
For the longest time
She thought he might not come.
The mist was stubborn to lift;
The organist—a lone buzzard
Struggled to find new tunes
And the bridesmaid gulls
Distressed the clifftop pews.

She married the wind on a Tuesday.
When he came, he was cold;
He tore tears from her eyes.
When she cried out, "I do,"
He ripped her words away
And threw them back from the cliffs.
Even the gulls and the buzzard
Knew to hold their peace.

She married the wind on a Tuesday.
The path up the cliff was steep
And he pulled at her dress,
Impatiently lewd, until the top,
Where she spread her arms,
Closed her eyes for his kiss
Then let her husband take her
Over the threshold.

First published in Dreams and Nightmares, *2005*

Narcissus

while word not last
        for each word in love
                wait for echo
        next
next

Ricki Grady

Ricki Grady is a freelance graphic designer from Oregon whose first book, Bebop Garden *was published by Dymaxicon in 2011. Ricki's passion for writing and gardening grew out of an association with a garden store for whom she designed a logo. She soon found herself writing their newsletters, and all of their print and TV advertising. In order to write about plants, she had to grow them herself, and that was when the gardening bug bit.*

Ricki joined the Hardy Plant Society of Oregon and began writing for their bulletin. Eschewing how-to books in her search for knowledge she turned instead to gardening literature, finding inspiration in Mirabel Osler's A Gentle Plea for Chaos *and Des Kennedy's* Crazy About Gardening*—the latter offering Ricki the revelation that the garden can be a very humorous place.*

These days Ricki lives in Portland, Oregon with her partner and two cats. She maintains two gardens and keeps the blog Sprig to Twig, *where she writes about her experiences and insights. Ricki is active in the Portland gardening community, exchanging ideas (and plants!) with fellow gardeners and gardening bloggers.*

Bebop Garden:
Introduction

Let me tell you 'bout
The birds and the bees
And the flowers and the trees
And the moon up above...
And a thing called love.
  ~ Jewel Akens

Dear Reader,

I share a fantasy with a lot of people: I see myself in a jazz band, so tuned in to my fellows that we can extemporize freely, taking a simple, familiar tune into unknown territory with wild abandon. There is one problem with this wishful vision: I have a tin ear. No amount of musical training or hours of practice can give me the vocabulary to speak music.

But in gardening I have found an improvisational

medium better suited to my talents. Jazzy compositions are no longer beyond me; they just get worked out by startling plant juxtapositions, rhythmic color repetitions, harmonic arrangements of light and shadow.

My life as a gardener began with a rubble-strewn lot adjacent to the old house my partner, Richard, and I were remodeling. A Japanese quince held court by the front stairs, ivy twined along the porch and a few yellow irises struggled valiantly against the death grip of morning glory vines. To top it off, the city had recently dug up our parking strip to install new curbs and left a patch of ugly dirt behind.

I had always directed my strong nesting urges toward beautification of interiors. Our family moved so often that sown seeds would never have had a chance to produce something recognizable before we were off to some new destination, and a bucket of paint and new towels for the bathroom were more appropriate fixes for temporary surroundings.

Even when, in 1968, my family landed in a charmingly ramshackle Victorian destined to become home for the next 11 years, it never occurred to me to address the outdoor space beyond mowing the grass—if that.

Single mom'ing two lively youngsters left little time for such diversions anyway. We did plant a vegetable garden one spring as a family project. It was fun, but a failure of sorts, as it did not make veggies any more appealing at the dinner table to Hillary or Din.

In its second season, the novelty having worn off, the garden languished from general neglect. By the third year it was abandoned altogether and quickly reverted to its original, weed-infested state. I am ashamed to admit we once received a notice from the city demanding we remove the "noxious vegetation" creating an eyesore for our neighborhood.

I was certainly not impervious to the delights of a beautiful garden, or to the profound effect flora might have on one's environment. In fact, I credit an extreme act of horticulture with propelling me from our cozy Victorian dwelling of so many years.

One day, returning home at noon, I was struck by an uncustomary brightness in the house. When I discovered the source—a laurel hedge we had depended upon to screen us from the slummy house next door had been lopped off close to the ground—I found myself in the grip of a temper tantrum the likes of which even divorce had failed to produce.

I was mobilized, fired by high dudgeon. Within the month we had moved to a completely different part of town.

Why am I telling you all of this? Just to let you know that gardening was certainly not in my genes. It had never risen to more than a blip on my radar screen. I think you would be hard-pressed to identify a less likely candidate for conversion to the Tao of gardening.

Skip ahead a few years to the scene I first described. Here we were, struggling to carve out a living space in the second floor of what had for years been an up-and-down duplex, replete with sagging acoustical tile ceilings and orange and green shag carpet. My love, Richard, has a background in design and construction. He was doing all of the heavy lifting where the remodel was concerned, so I thought it only made sense to give him free rein with the fun design decisions as well.

What to do with my need to have an effect on my surroundings? With little gardening experience (you might even agree that my few brushes with the art had been more negative than positive) and virtually no money to spend, I took my nesting instincts outdoors. At the time, I had no intention of taking over the entire vacant lot, and certainly not of turning it into a garden that would stop traffic and delight passers-by. I just wanted to have a few flowers I could pick to bring into the house.

Ten years later, I know the Latin names of most of the plants in my garden (pronunciation is still a struggle). I also know that a garden can happen without a major investment of dollars.

Time, labor, and imagination are a different story. Most gardeners will tell you the time spent in the garden is a lot like meditation: it refreshes and renews. The labor is excellent exercise. You will save health club dues and never again find yourself checking your watch to see how many more minutes you promised yourself you would spend on the Stairmaster. I lose myself in the garden: digging, weeding, bending, carrying and reaching. By the end of the day I can feel it in every muscle, but I never give it a thought at the time. Often, nightfall is my only indication it must be time to quit. Or, more frequently, Richard will lure me with a glass of wine and a gentle reminder to get cleaned up if we want to make it to that movie. A hot bubble bath never felt better than at the end of a good workout in the garden.

What I really want to do, in writing about gardening,

is convey the wide spectrum of pleasures it makes available. A great sense of community, so sadly lacking in the modern world, swirls around you as soon as you pick up a trowel. Becoming an active participant in the great web of life overtakes you, even if your gardening is confined to a windowsill. The ageism and sexism known to creep stealthily into so many of life's arenas are resoundingly absent. Male or female, you can garden at any age. You will be valued for your enthusiasm at the early stages; as you mature, you will be valued for your wisdom and experience.

The imagination takes flight, even if you thought yours was in short supply. Whimsical constructs and irreverent use of oddball objects that would seem ridiculous in the house take on a peculiar charm outdoors. Almost no wild idea is too bizarre to bring special individuality to a space and make it sing your own song.

A sense of humor is perhaps your best asset when trying something new. If it brings a smile to your face or, better yet, elicits a giggle, you can be sure you are on the right track. If it pleases your eye, other eyes will linger there as well. A particularly outrageous installation might attract some caustic remarks. So what? Even a lush bed of regal hostas has been known to prompt snobbish snorts of disapproval from opinionated experts.

The world is full of rules and guidelines for garden design if you care about such things. It never hurts to read up on any subject, just so you will know what rules you are breaking.

Breaking rules is, after all, how most art happens. Anarchy in the garden is a harmless form of indulgence.

As you go about your liberated way, trusting your instincts, your inner artist will begin to express itself, bringing you untold gratification. Just remember: there is no one "right way." The right way is your way.

I will be the first to admit that some of what you read here may sound like zealotry. Of late, we have been dealing with end-of-life issues with our last surviving parent and it has taken an emotional toll. The garden has been a refuge, a comfort, and an outlet for pent-up feelings, and has taken on greater meaning than it had before. It's difficult to express just what that meaning is, for it is elusive and enigmatic, as are the feelings with which we grapple.

In some sense, all gardens are healing gardens. They open a door to the unconscious. As we busy ourselves with the minutia of maintenance, our souls are freed to range around in unknown territory.

Most emphatically, regardless of the scale of your undertaking, remember that the fortune you could easily spend might ultimately detract from your enjoyment. Plants with a history (you grew it from seed, you traded for it, it was a gift, it is a memorial) give pleasure or solace beyond their appealing presence in the soil.

Gardening is all process. Thinking of it that way will help you live in the here and now. You will thrill to the small moments of perfection. You will sidestep the frustration of a grand plan's refusal to be fully realized.

I recently heard a seemingly profound piece of advice from a pundit on a radio show: When you take on a task in the garden, do just that one thing. Carry only the tool for that specific chore, and do not allow yourself to be sidetracked by other tasks crying out for attention.

Sounded good, so I gave it a shot. No dice. Such a program might work for cleaning house, where efficiency gets the job done quickly so we can move on to more enjoyable pastimes. In the garden, all of the little distractions are what add up to the joy and wonderment of the gardening experience.

Efficiency in the garden is something to be avoided, for you may miss out on some quirky sight, sound, smell, or event—perhaps a shaft of light illuminating a plant combination you had never particularly noticed before, rustling grasses in a breeze, a heady whiff of flowering tobacco at dusk, or a territorial dispute at the bird feeder.

Any subject introduced in this book can be studied in depth, approached from a scholarly point of view and enlarged upon to fill volumes on its own. I have chosen to treat it all in a more casual, conversational style, much as I approach it myself. Most of what I have to share is anecdotal, based on personal experience, trial and error and ten years of bumbling along just following my own nose.

I made a lot of mistakes, but I also made discoveries that might help you make a garden without breaking the bank. In the process, you are apt to find a lifetime distraction, or at least a pleasant hobby, to constantly enrich your experience in ways both predictable and unexpected.

Yours distractedly,
Ricki Grady

Cindy Lee Berryhill

Born and raised in Los Angeles, Cindy Lee Berryhill is a singer-songwriter and has been identified with the New York City Anti-folk movement, along with artists such as Beck and Michelle Shocked. Her debut album, Who's Gonna Save The World? *was released in October 1987 and was followed by* Naked Movie Star *in 1989. Her third album,* Garage Orchestra, *earned a four-star review from* Rolling Stone, *and was followed a year later by the album* Straight Outta Marysville.

In 1995 her fiancé, the rock writer Paul Williams, suffered a brain injury and Cindy Lee has spent much of her time over the past 17 years caring for him. During this time Cindy Lee wrote her first novel, Memoirs of a Female Messiah, *which was published by Entwhistle Books in 1999, and released her fifth and sixth albums,* Living Room *and* Beloved Stranger.

Since September 2009 Cindy Lee has been writing a blog at cindyleeberryhill.com, *where she documents her experiences of living with Paul's brain injury. She is currently at work on her seventh album.*

When She Left Picasso,

the days were still warm, all the world was young
it was summer
or what was left of it.

When she left Picasso
there was nothing to be done to make the going easy
she was met at the end of the lane
by a man with a lamp
who showed her the way out
and which road to go
away from Picasso.

When she left Picasso
she couldn't eat or sleep
there was too little time
there was too far to go
and the future a steep/grade up/into the unknown.

When she left Picasso
it was a summer night
with the windows of the town fully open with light
and the terrible red eye of Antares staring down
from the bright net of stars called Scorpio.

And, what was there to be done with
the things he'd given her
the stories, the visions,
the children of nuclear fission
it was a hell of a way to go...

...when she left Picasso,
he wondered why

wanted to know the ways a bird can fly
so many had flown too close to the sun
but she has left me while our love was still young
and that rattled the soul of old Picasso.

When she left Picasso
the waves smashed on the shore
in the south of France
the rip tide was great
and pulled at full force
full of yearning for Picasso.

When she left,
and they kissed their last kiss
white hot as the first
he slammed his fist on the desk
spilling the green tea,
'women don't leave a man like me,
don't you know who I am, I'm Picasso.'

When she left Picasso
god he was mad
all the colors drained out of the room
and left were the etchings of structures of things
like bones and stones and tombs,
and the sucking black hole
at the end of the o, in Picasso.

When she left Picasso
she wasn't afraid
she had the right of the spheres on her side,
and the winds blew behind her and tousled her hair
and the gods in her did confide,
'we'd hoped you'd stay for a while,
but if you must then go,
you've earned your wings
with this Picasso.'

When she left
started her car
set the GPS for somewhere,
all the way down that long-haul road
were scattered bones of those that had gone before
lovers friends and foe of Picasso.

When she left Picasso
the Santa Anas were blowing
from California to Barcelona
the tin roofs of bordellos were coming down,
a chime from a church bell
the doppler'd harmonica
the sound of his voice,
his voice that echoed through her lost mining towns,
on the winds of desire that blew through the portals
of the P and o, of Picasso.

When she left Picasso
goodbye was still a hello
a fond waiting 'til next text or talk on the phone
every door left open
and buttons undone
like a nuclear wasteland
with all things in place
but the humans were totally gone.
Like this she said yes, to life and to love
and sent a wish out into the unknown
a kiss to all things
both fierce and beautiful
like this, she said no, to Picasso.

For No Good Reason

Every day another one falls off the Earth
with little time to say goodbye.
Today another one,
and I'm afraid I'll never see you again,
with no chance to tell you
how deeply you've touched me
despite all the walls,
how you've reached me

It's not an easy task.
Ours was not made for life's long journeys,
because you live in winter
and I in San Diego,
with nowhere to go.
Still the hunger, the feelings prevail
for no good reason....

How do you say it
when it lives in waves not particles
it wanders streets
and doesn't live in homes
the feeling grows
for no good reason.

A thunderous cloudburst breaks the air
lightning from the dark heart of a storm
and the walls come down.

What are the things I haven't told you?
That I love you?
That flowers spring up at our footfall.
That the colors of your canvas excites me.
That all my cells sing hallelujah.
That, despite the gaping chasm between us, the ridiculous
enthusiasm lingers on, thrives even, for
some no good, god-forsaken reason

Mark Eagleton

Mark Eagleton is a thirty-year old writer from Queensland, Australia who opted out of formal education in 2002 to work as a hotel housekeeper, and later travel and document his experiences. He recently spent four months living in Ho Chi Minh City, Vietnam, socializing with the locals and making extensive notes of the conversations he had in preparation for the novel he is currently writing. Mark is drawn to exploring the dark and desperate side of life that most of us are uncomfortable with, and shy away from. He finds himself mentally inhabiting the lives of people who have suffered great pain or loss, much as an actor does, and thus much of his work is written in the first person.

You can read more of Mark's stories on his tumblr blog, shakespeareverdidthis. When not writing, Mark reads extensively and cultivates an obsession for Italian horror movies, Asian cinema, and periodically, comic books. He currently lives in the Sunshine Coast region in a small apartment by the beach with his girlfriend and their cat. Broken *is Mark's first published work.*

Broken

Five Vignettes

i) Behind Their Smiles

The police took my father's computer and then later, they took him. The newspaper and television reporters said there were over two thousand pornographic pictures of children on my father's computer.

My mother hid in her bedroom, and we heard her crying into her pillow, her sobs muffled and distant. My sister and I sat in the living room watching TV together. We didn't want to hear what they were saying about Dad, but we couldn't look away either. They were talking about someone else. "Geoff Campbell, a respected member of the community" was not our father.

Our father was a good man who loved us and who helped us with our homework and cheered for me at my weekend football games. Geoff Campbell was a guy who sat in a dark room looking at child pornography, and who covered his face with a jacket when the police led him into the station.

Our father told us he loved us each night before bed and reminded us to say our prayers and to ask Jesus to forgive us our sins. On Sundays my father's voice rang out loud and clear above all others as he sang in church, his big warm hand resting lightly on my shoulder.

When we went back to school, everyone looked at my sister and me as if we were carrying some deadly disease. The teachers treated us with caution, as though we were suddenly fragile, damaged. Our friends avoided us. We scared them. Something dark and evil had entered our lives and no one wanted a part of it.

After a week our mother didn't make us go to school anymore. She stayed in her room and took the pills the doctor prescribed. Her eyes were red from crying, and whenever she spoke her voice was hesitant and broken, as if she were learning a new language. The truth is she had no idea how to describe the new world she was living in. None of us did.

When Geoff Campbell was released on bail he knocked on our front door and stood there staring at his shoes, looking lost, like the stranger he had become. He put his hand on my head and rustled my hair, but his touch felt awkward and unfamiliar. Who was this new man, the one who had ruined all our lives? I didn't know what to say to him. My mother locked her bedroom door and refused to come out. My sister hovered in the background, pretending to be preoccupied with her cell phone.

That night Geoff Campbell slept in the spare bedroom next to mine, and I heard him praying out loud, his voice frantic. I thought about going to him, but I was scared. I didn't know what to say, or what to do.

We stayed in our rooms as much as possible that week, my sister and I sending each other text messages. We wondered what was going to happen—not just to him, but to us.

My sister found the note on the kitchen table. In it my father wrote of how much he loved us all, and how deeply sorry he was for the mess he had made of our lives. *I have given into weakness and must stand before the Lord in judgment*, he wrote. I remember that line in particular.

The police took the letter, and a few days later they found Geoff Campbell's broken body at the bottom of a cliff. After that he wasn't in the news anymore. Our mother sold the house, and we moved away and started a new life together. It was not a bad life.

But even now I wonder what goes on in the houses next to ours. I wonder what evil the neighbors are hiding behind their smiles. There is a great darkness in people's hearts, and I look for it everywhere.

ii) Letters From My Brother

From time to time I receive letters from my brother in the mail. Whenever I see that familiar envelope in the bottom of my mailbox I get a sick feeling in my stomach and know that I will be depressed and anxious for the next few days. It is as though he waits for me to forget all about him and then, at the opportune moment, he reaches out of his dark closet and slaps me hard across the face.

It is the same every time. I hold the yellow, government-issued envelope in my shaky hand and immediately become clammy with sweat. I think about throwing it in the bin, unopened. I tell myself this is what I am going to do. I am going to throw it away. But I put it on the kitchen table, and it sits there all day.

And all day I tell myself not to think about it, to pretend it's not there. I watch TV and try my best to concentrate on what is happening on the screen, but the letter is always in the back of my mind, and I find myself thinking about things I do not want to think about.

When I finally can't take it anymore, I tear the envelope open and take out the carefully folded pages with my brother's bad handwriting printed on them. My heart is beating like someone is holding a gun to my head. I stand there breathing heavily, and then I begin to read. It is always as though my brother is writing from some place known only to him, another world.

Dear Mick, he will have written. It is always the same. It never changes.

When he was a year old I carried him on my shoulders, my little brother, and I held him high for the world to see.

Dear Mick, the drugs make it difficult to string a proper thought together. There are things I try to think about but then I lose track of my thoughts and I've lost them. It happens just like that. The place is the same. I'm getting lost all the time. They are always changing things here. The hallways always lead to some place they didn't lead to yesterday.

When I ask the doctors about this, they pretend they don't know what I'm talking about. But they know.

I haven't seen my brother's face in almost five years. I would like to say I remember him as a boy, that when I think about him I remember something good.

I can't say these things.

When I think about my brother, the image that comes to mind is his face on the news as he was led, cuffed, from the courthouse to a waiting police car. His hair was too long and when he looked into the camera lens there was the hint of a smirk on his face, a dullness that made me think of a person without a soul, an empty vessel.

If you opened him up, I thought, there'd be nothing but blackness inside.

...If they didn't put drugs in the water and if the air conditioning didn't pump secret gasses into the air I could explain things better. But my mind is so clouded.

If only you would come here and see what they are doing, you would understand. You wouldn't believe the things they say about me. I could tell you things, and you would know it was truth.

You are the only person I can trust. They are watching everything I do. They are reading this. Maybe they will change the words I write. I don't know. They change everything here.

"Evil Personified." This is one of the headlines from that time. Red letters leaping out at me from the front page. He showed no emotions in the courtroom, they said. No remorse.

I stopped reading the newspapers, stopped watching the news altogether. I moved overseas for a while. I lived the life of a person with no ties. I had no family, no history. A blank slate. When I finally left the earth I would leave nothing behind, no traces of my existence.

Sometimes I remembered that this new life was a fiction I'd created for myself. A false history. I had a brother. A million miles away was another human being who shared the same blood as me. And as much as I wanted to deny this, there was no hiding the truth from myself.

...Sometimes I think about Mum and Dad. I think about what life must be like for them now. I know they are not dead.

They took them for a reason. The replaced them with actors, clones of some sort. At first I thought they were robots, that they weren't human. But they were just people playing a role.

They thought I wouldn't notice. That I couldn't tell the difference. But I knew. I heard things. I heard whispered conversations late at night when they thought I was sleeping. And I saw looks on their faces when they thought I wasn't paying attention.

If you had seen them you would have known too. How could you not know?

I have to find out what happened to them. They have hidden them somewhere and it is your job to find them. When you do, we will all be together again.

When I run into people I used to know, old friends or those who used to know my parents, I always do my best not to look at them. If I keep my eyes on the ground or pretend to be interested in something else, sometimes— if I am lucky—they will pass me by.

There are times when a meeting can't be helped, and I can't escape the expression on their faces. It's a look I've gotten to know well over the years. When their eyes meet mine there is a fear there.

They look at me and an expression of complete dismay appears on their faces. They try to hide it, but it's always there. Just the sight of me makes people think about stuff they never want to think about. When I meet people from that time they are forced to remember murder and death and blood, and they can't get away from me fast enough.

I don't blame them for feeling that way. I experience the same feeling each day. I will be leaning over the sink, washing my hands or brushing my teeth, and my eyes will lock on my reflection and it all comes rushing over me and I am suddenly weak at the knees.

If I could, I'd run away from myself so fast nothing could catch me. I'd run and never stop. I imagine that if I move fast enough and never stop moving I'll come as close to not existing as I can get.

iii) Without a Trace

I was fifteen the year my sister disappeared. She went out to a nightclub with friends and no one ever saw her again. Afterwards, my parents were forever changed. They stopped smiling, and when I came home from school the house was always quiet. My mother spent her days in bed watching TV, smoking cigarettes, and crying a lot. Her eyes were always red.

Later, I discovered she was on some pretty strong medication to calm her nerves. When I was older I'd steal a few of her pills and my friends and I would wash them down with beer at whatever party we were at on the weekend.

The pills made me feel as though I was floating around wrapped in pink cotton candy. It was a good feeling, and sometimes I would get the sensation that my spirit was leaving my body. I would actually feel it go up and out, through my chest. Up near the ceiling I would look down at my body, and sometimes I got scared that a strong wind would blow my spirit too far away and I would be lost out there, in the atmosphere, forever.

When life was normal my sister would drive my best friend, David, and me to our friends' places; she would let us smoke in her car and buy us alcohol. "Don't tell the parentals," she would tell us. We drove with the windows down and rap music up so loud we couldn't hear each other talk. And then she was gone.

My father spent a lot of time reading the Bible. He stayed up late at the kitchen table reading and drinking coffee. I think he was waiting for my sister to come home or waiting for a call from the police. I think he expected her to just come walking in the front door one night, like she had been on a long holiday or something. We would gather around her, me and my mother and father, and we would smother her with hugs. No one would be angry with her for being gone so long. Then things would go back to normal.

After she disappeared, I would frequently check my sister's Facebook page, looking for any sign of her, but the only new posts were from her friends telling her how much they loved and missed her. After a while her friends stopped writing, and there were no new posts.

Sometimes I thought about writing her a message myself, but I never did. I would sit there, my hands hovering just above the keyboard, but my fingers couldn't move and I never knew what to say to her anyway.

For the first six months or so, my sister's boyfriend visited our house all the time. He spent a lot of time talking to my father in a low voice, and I never heard what they talked about. But I knew they were talking about my sister. Later, I understood they were talking about how the police hadn't found anything.

Once, after he stopped coming around, I saw him at the shopping center with a new girlfriend. They were holding hands, and when he saw me he smiled and raised his hand at me. I walked straight past him, my heart throbbing in my chest, and as I walked I thought about how good it would feel to tear his body limb from limb with my bare hands.

Later, David and I drove to his house and stabbed his tires with a steak knife. Afterwards I felt better, but not that much better.

Now I don't think about her that often. But sometimes I find myself wondering what my sister would look like now, or how her life might have turned out. And I think about all the ways all our lives would be different.

It happens at odd times. I will be driving on the highway somewhere, and she will just pop into my head. I'll remember being in her car with the music up loud, smoking cigarettes, singing along. At that moment I experience an empty feeling in my stomach; I know that this is how my parents feel all the time.

Sometimes I get scared knowing I live in a world where people can just vanish without a trace. That one minute you can be dancing with your friends, and the next it's as if you never existed at all.

iv) Far From Here

When my wife is in the shower and I am still in bed pretending to be asleep, I masturbate slowly beneath the sheet. I am not thinking about her. I am not thinking about anything in particular. When my semen is a warm pool on my stomach, I let it sit there until it gets cool. Then I smear it into my skin and leave it there to dry. When my wife gets out of the shower to get dressed for work, I pretend I am asleep.

She puts on her clothes and I do not move. I just listen.

A long time ago I would have watched her get dressed. I would have talked to her, said something, maybe made us breakfast. But now I keep my eyes closed until I hear the car engine start and the sound of the garage door rolling up. When the garage door closes and I can no longer hear the car, I know it is safe to open my eyes.

In the bathroom I study my reflection for changes in my appearance. Lately, I have become concerned with the ageing process. Are these lines near my eyes new? Were they there yesterday?

I cannot remember.

I think about using something sharp to cut around the edges of my face so I can pull the skin away. I am almost certain that if I were to do this there would be a new face beneath the old one.

I feel the existence of a stranger beneath my skin, and I know he is watching me always and listening to the things I say. I try to speak as little as possible, but I worry this stranger can read my mind and this scares me, because I don't know if he is my friend or my enemy.

I do not know what his intentions are.

Naked in the kitchen, I mix scotch and ginger ale and use it to wash down my medication. My medication is for anxiety. These days lots of people have anxiety. It is nothing to be ashamed of. My doctor told me this. *It is nothing to be ashamed of*, he said.

Sometimes, I think about all the people walking around shopping centers, driving in cars, and I wonder how many of them have anxiety, and how many of them are on medications like mine. There are all these people out there; they are afraid all the time but they don't know what it is they are afraid of. Thinking these things gives me a feeling of reassurance.

I watch *Dr. Phil* during the day. I download new episodes and watch them with my scotch and dry; sometimes I imagine that my wife and I are on his show and he is sitting in-between us on his tall stool.

There is something wrong with you, he says to me.

Dr. Phil is a very wise man and I nod my head at him in agreement. When I look at my wife she is crying and looking at her lap. Dr. Phil passes her a box of tissues and she dries her eyes.

When my wife comes home from work I do not recognize her. *Who is this woman*, I think. This is something that happens often—I know this is my wife, but I'm sure that it really isn't. I don't know why this happens.

I look at her a long time before saying anything. She is standing beside the couch where I am sitting with my scotch. I look up at her and say, *who are you?*

I need a drink, she says and leaves me there. Dr. Phil is talking to a woman who cannot control her children and he is speaking to her in firm soothing tones. I would like for someone to talk to me in this way.

In the kitchen I hear her ice striking the bottom of a glass, and for a while it echoes through my skull with some hidden message I can't quite decipher.

v) Sometimes I Think About Breaking All the Windows

Before she was killed in a car accident my wife used to tell me she believed there was something cold in me. She would say there was an untouchable part of me, that at times I could be distant and emotionally vacant.

Needless to say, I didn't take these statements as compliments and retired to my study to fume in silence. That was a long time ago now, before the accident.

Lately though, I've been thinking about those times and about something that happened then. I was living the kind of suburban life I'd promised myself I would never live. But there I was, watering the front lawn in the late afternoon. I was even enjoying it, I think. I had become one of those guys who "took pride in his lawn."

The afternoon peace was pierced by the sound of glass shattering from the house next door. I didn't take much notice at first, but when the sound repeated itself a few more times I dropped the hose on the grass and wandered out to the street to get a good look.

My neighbour, a grey haired man in his late forties, came into view carrying a hammer in a clenched fist. His face appeared deep purple in the fading light. I watched as he shattered all the windows on the front of his house then withdrew to the middle of his yard to admire his handy work.

He looked satisfied, standing there with his hands on his hips, his back to me. I remember thinking that he looked like a man who had gone to battle with his home and won convincingly.

"I'm calling the police." It was Mrs Deboree from across

the street. She'd been watering the lawn too. Her retired husband, Brian, was by the front door sitting in a fold out chair, drinking from a can of beer. "I'm calling the police," she called again, her voice growing shrill.

Our grey haired neighbour turned slowly to face us. "Excuse me?"

"I'm calling the police," she said again.

"I don't know if I'm wrong, tell me if I'm wrong, but this is my house. Am I wrong?" He looked at me. "Am I wrong?"

"No, I think you have a point," I told him. There were other things I might have said, but I could see where he was coming from and, truthfully, I was curious to see where this situation was headed.

"Thank you," he said. "This is my house. These are my windows. This is my place."

"You can't go destroying it," she said. "You can't go smashing up the neighbourhood because you own something."

"Can't I? I think that's exactly what ownership means. This is my place."

"You—"

"Honey, leave him be. I think it's over now," Brian Deboree said, deciding that now was the time to add his part. He spoke in calm and deliberate tones, as though he were a judge who had come to a verdict after much thought.

She ignored him. "I'm calling the police."

"I was in the war," the man said. "I was in the war."

"I don't think that gives—"

"I was in the war and this is my place. I'll do what I please with it. I'll do as I please." He sounded close to tears now, defeated and desperate.

And we stood there. We stood there, and no one said a thing. There wasn't anything else to say; it had all been said. We'd only be saying the same things over and over, maybe with different words, but probably with the same ones. I suppose we could have said other things, but they were hard to say, and we were not the kind of people who said difficult things.

When I think about this, I think that this is what my wife may have meant when she told me that there was something cold and unbreakable in me. And maybe—despite my fuming silences—I understood her back then. But that was before the accident, and before everything that could be broken in a man was broken in me.

Walt Foreman

Walt Foreman has an MA in creative writing from the Writing Seminars at Johns Hopkins, and an MFA in Screen and Television Writing from the School of Cinema-Television at the University of Southern California. He has had short stories published in Ploughshares, Ontario Review, Clackamas Literary Review, Baltimore Review, *and* Eclipse; *his novel,* Fairy Tale, *was published in 2003 by Baskerville Publishers.*

In 2006 Walt sold a feature screenplay, Duck Stuck, *and he recently signed a distribution deal for* Sparkle and Tooter, *an indie feature film that he wrote, produced, directed, and edited.*

Walt Foreman's short story collection, Beer in the Sun *from which the two stories appearing here are taken, will be published by Dymaxicon later this year. Presently he is working on a PhD in creative writing at Georgia State University, where he has an assistantship.*

Lulu

I walked down to the boulevard. I bought a bottle of Cristal and bestowed it upon a transient. Tears of sand flowed from his eyes when he drank. What do you think? I said, but he wouldn't say. Earthquakes and riots came and went, people fucked and laughed and married and died, the transient finished the bottle and relieved me of his company. I watched the traffic.

The scarred day bloomed into night. A prostitute stood beside me. She was young but the backs of her thighs were moon fields of cellulite. I wondered if Lulu had cellulite. I wanted to tell her I didn't care, that it would make me no difference if all her privates were Argus and would stare at me as I loved them. Lulu had banished me to the world, and the world without Lulu meant no more to me than the most bootless part of a mote. She the girl of my dreams, incony lambent smile, and a wit. She had a wit, I had seen it, it was wondrous.

The prostitute crossed the street and sat on the bench by the bus stop. I wondered how she thought she was going to make any money that way, sitting immobile on a bench, not walking or gamboling or in any way revealing her industry. She crossed and uncrossed her cellulite, smoothed the hem of her dress and crossed her arms. She took out a cigarette from her purse, put it back, took it back out and lit it. A shadow of pink neon bled into her face and she frowned and brushed it away. A Taurus pulled up by the bench. She stood and the car absorbed her and drove away.

I went to the tar pits. I went to a museum. A winsome blond man of twenty or so passed on the sidewalk, method-acting the part of a lunatic. A voice lilted around the corner and I hurried my step to look but it was someone else.

I went to a pier. It was nighttime and gold-crested waves were arriving from a million years ago and breaking on the beach. There were Ferris wheels and restaurants and a blue metal sign that read, *No Jumping From Bridge or Pier*; there were mountains in the distance, their feet stippled with light. A beautiful black man played a wooden flute and rode a bicycle. I climbed a dark Ferris wheel and threw peanuts at the fishermen but they ignored me. I jumped off the wheel and flew out miles into the darkness to where it was quiet and all I could hear were the waves. I swam to the bottom of the sea and waited for my Lulu.

Chez Motel Six

I was living in a Motel Six. (Tom Bodett has likely never done this.) I had come back from teaching English to four-year-olds in Korea with no job and no money, having spent all the money I made teaching club-hopping till dawn in Seoul every weekend with Army brats and diplomats' kids twenty years younger than me, beautiful girls and boys who looked on me as something of an avuncular figure, or perhaps simply an amusing loser who had missed his time and was trying desperately to get it back. When I got into Nashville, a man twenty-five years my senior was waiting on me at the airport. I got into his Lincoln Continental and he drove me to his large house in Brentwood and helped me with my things to his guest room. His name was Pete and he had made his fortune in insurance but now wrote full-time, four hours a day he liked to brag, in an office he rented in a glass building on Franklin Road. He had expensive paintings in his dining and living rooms, including a minimalist abstract that I am sure meant no more to Pete than it did to me; all the bathrooms and the kitchen were marble; the kitchen alone was bigger than most of the apartments I had ever lived in. In the daytime I would go out and look for a job and an apartment, and at night Pete's wife would cook for the three of us and we would have a pleasant meal in their expensive dining room, after which Pete would herd me to the den, where he would show me his extensive collection of books by epigone writers, ask me all about my opinions on writing and finally give me something he had written to read. He was estranged from his only daughter, and after I had been there a week he turned on me suddenly in a pleasant conversation and suggested, with a glass of rum and Coke in his hand and an abrupt bitterness in his tone, that I find somewhere else to live. I had just told him that I thought the novel he was working on was somewhat unoriginal, that I thought he could do better.

I checked into the motel at seven in the evening. I found my room, first floor on the back side, deposited my suitcase and my overnight bag on the floor, stripped down to nothing and masturbated while looking in the mirror, thought briefly about killing myself, asked God to forgive me for masturbating, took a nap, took a shower and went out to the Denny's by the interstate for an omelet. I was back in the room by nine-thirty. I played my trombone for a few minutes until someone in the next room banged on the wall. At ten minutes after ten I called a studio trombone player I had taken lessons from years before while I was in college and asked him if he knew any band directors looking for private trombone teachers. When I told him I was living in a motel, he said that he and another trombone player I had met once were going out to a microbrewery on West End for a couple beers, and why didn't I join them? So I brushed my teeth at my motel room sink and put on my faded windbreaker that bore, along with my name and instrument, the name of the marching band I had been a member of in college, and went out of the room and got into the '77 Datsun Coupe I had bought with the last of my Korea money and drove to the brewery.

It was a weeknight and by the time I got there the place was nearly empty. Hal (the guy I had called) bought me two Guinness replicas, and he and Stu made great efforts to include me in their conversation and make me feel like one of them. I had subbed once a couple years out of college for Hal, but it was a marginal gig with a stage band made up mostly of skilled amateurs and we had both known that it was a token gesture because I had paid him forty bucks for a lesson, had paid him forty bucks a few times, and I didn't quite have what it took and he no doubt felt bad about taking the money of someone who said he would like to play in town but wasn't going to be doing so. So they talked about playing and musicians they played with regularly and tried to pretend I was one of them and it was obvious they were being nice to me so I wouldn't kill myself out of despair from living in a Motel Six but I was glad to be with people nonetheless and was even able to laugh several times at things they said that were remotely clever. I looked about a few times to see if there were any beautiful Southern women present but there were only three people in the place besides us, a guy about my age drinking by himself on the other side of the bar, the bartender, and a waitress who came out twice from the kitchen to talk to the bartender. The waitress wasn't cute but she nonetheless hurried back into the kitchen the second time when she saw me looking at her and didn't appear again. By then the place was closing and Hal paid for his and my beers and Stu paid for his and we went out to the parking lot.

They were parked next to each other, a Subaru wagon and a Toyota Corolla. I had parked my Datsun further down the lot in the irrational thought that I might leave before them and they might not see me getting in it; one of the brewery's outside lights was falling on it and illuminating the rust holes in the body, the smashed headlight, the missing hubcaps. It reminded me of a time in my youth when I had seen losers in coffee-grinders on the interstate and how I had thought then that I would never be the forty-year-old guy driving the worst car on the road. Hal was telling a joke as the three of us lingered by the shiny new Subaru and the shiny new Corolla.

"So this queer and this football player are in a bar, and the queer says to the football player that he'll bet him a hundred bucks that he can beat him in football. So the football player just laughs at him, but the queer says, No, this is different, you play differently. We both drink a beer at the same time and whoever belches first gets a touchdown. Then you pull down your pants and fart for the extra point. So the football player says, a hundred bucks? The queer says, a hundred bucks. So the football player buys them both beers and they drink the beers at the same time. The football player belches, pulls down his pants to fart and the queer pulls down his pants and grabs the football player from behind and says, Block that kick! Block that kick!"

They both laughed and smiled at me and I was annoyed that one or both of them had designs on me sexually in the midst of my living in a motel but of course I couldn't be sure and then I thought that maybe I was just paranoid, though both men and women had always come on to me at the worst possible times in my life, perhaps it was biological to the species, see a wounded specimen and try to mate with it. The only specimens that interested me, i.e. supermodels between the ages of eighteen and twenty-three, rarely if ever came on to me, while less-than-beautiful women, and men in general, both gay and seemingly straight, seemed impelled by a hidden law to do so. Fortunately, now I was losing my hair and it would not much longer be an issue. I thought to myself that Hal had made a gesture of genuine, unrequired human kindness and that I was hopelessly egotistical and neurotic. I thought of the few times in my life that really beautiful men or women had hit on me. There was the time when I was in the Army and stationed at Fort Knox, and I was in the tiny town of Radcliffe's one Subway on a gray late-winter afternoon and a breathtaking girl—she might have been seventeen—with *fleur-de-lis* lips and pomegranate temples leaned on the counter very close to me and, with an impishly feminine sigh, told me how tired she was; there was the time I was standing outside a bar in the Itaewon district of Seoul at four in the morning and a modelesque, tall man of perhaps twenty with straight blonde hair told me that Whitman was his favorite poet before giving me his hotel name and room number on a napkin. Stu said something to Hal about a gig the two of them were playing soon and they bid me goodbye and went to their respective cars and got in, and I was alone again. I walked across the well-lit parking lot to my rusting Datsun that shuddered whenever I went into first gear from a stop. The thought came to me that I could go back to the motel and watch pornos and beat off again, but then I thought that that might really do me in and so I got into the car and drove twenty miles down I-65 to the Waffle House at the Murfreesboro Road exit, knowing that there would be people there and that maybe I could hit it off with one of the waitresses and they would let me stay till the morning.

James Franco

Born and raised in the heart of Silicon Valley, James Franco is best known to the world as an actor. Less publicized is his career in the literary world as a writer and a teacher. James earned an MFA in creative writing from NYU's Brooklyn College while simultaneously studying poetry at North Carolina's prestigious Warren Wilson College. His first book, Palo Alto, *a collection of short stories based on his teenage years in the Bay Area, was published in 2010 by Scribner; his writing has appeared in* Esquire, The Wall Street Journal, *and* McSweeney's.

While undertaking his MFA James Franco also studied film making at NYU's Tisch School of the Arts, directing several films based on poetry. His film inspired by the controversial poem 'Herbert White' by Frank Bidart was premiered at Stanford University in March 2011, with the poet in attendance. James has since taught a course at NYU on modifying poetry into short films, combining two areas of passion for the writer/actor/director.

James is currently studying for a PhD at Yale University, while continuing to act, and to write. The Best of The Smiths *is his first collection of poetry to be published.*

The Best of The Smiths

Side A: "Erica and Sterling"

1. There is a Light that Never Goes Out

Please don't drop me home
Because it's not my home, it's their
Home, and I'm welcome no more

I waited in the shadow of my stupid house.
The mustang rolled up in the low black water,
Growling softly, then it stopped and purred.
Dark green paint like a deep flavor,
Like hard, sour-apple candy catching in my throat.

A hint of his blond swoop, the red button of his cigarette.
Smoke out the window. Sterling:
His name like a sword reflecting light in a dark room.
I'm the sword swallower.

And the grass licked my shoes.

2. Please, Please, Please

For once in my life
Let me get what I want
Lord knows, it would be the first time.

Now the picture had him in it
Up the red path
To my house
In his coal tux
Slicked like a wet cat.
I did my best in a lime green dress.

He still had friends at school,
Inside they all had some from his flask,
And he smiled a toothy smile, yellow and sharp.

And then we danced.
Not to one song, but ten songs.
It was the scene where the audience came over to my side,
Because I got what I wanted.

I was in love with a cliché.

Boys his age have bodies like knives.
I was holding one by the blade.

3. Ask

Shyness is nice, and
Shyness can stop you
From doing all the things in life
That you'd like to

I used to think about playing guitar,
Now I just listen.

With girls,
Just push and it gets there.
As soon as you hit puberty, go.
Take what comes, ugly is okay too.

With Erica, you were on someone's brother's bed
Pothead Mormons—listen—
A flower-covered comforter, blue ground;
A drum kit in the corner of the room,
Bass drum like a bulldog and a couple of sleeping flamingo
cymbals.

Gentle, but you weren't.
Love came—like viscosity filling a tube—
And you killed it with a bunch of thrusts.

Right in the middle she had to leave.
The second time she was better. Boring.

In the bathroom I sat naked on the floor.
Blood blooming.
—Science and fiction.
This is the rite of passage.
I am the vessel.
He is the instrument.

4. Stop me if You Think That You've Heard This One Before

I still love you
...only slightly, only slightly less than I used to

When I was in seventh grade I put kids in three categories:
Sports kids, smart kids, and social kids.

Some kids played football well and were dumb and ugly,
Some kids got great grades and their only friends were their
    parents,
There were others that danced among us

And made us all look like the kids we were.
They were big, daring, and sexual.
I wasn't much in any of the categories.

But in high school I met Sterling and I had something.

At this one party I was drunk and so was everyone else.
The sofas and chairs were floating,
And the people were shifting in their spheres,
I sat on a couch and took a ride.

Through a door to the kitchen, I saw a circus.
Plenty of colors: red and yellow and white.
There were a few ringmasters barking out things
And some lions in green letterman jackets
And this huge black seal, bonking down on this one guy,
    Ivan.
Bouncing him like he was a ball of air.
Until Ivan was slouched halfway to the linoleum.

One of the others hit him on the crown with a frying pan,
Like a cartoon, Ivan went all the way down and lay flat.

Sterling was on the side of it all.
Pouring foamy, piss-colored beer over Ivan's bloody pale face,
Laughing his electric eel grin,
With his sharp dogteeth.

On the car ride home,
He drove us drunk through the dark
Like a boat
On a flat, starless sea.

5. Girlfriend in a Coma

I know—it's really serious

Megan McKenna had a skinhead boyfriend,
He crashed his car into a pole.
The paramedics lifted her out of the crumpled car,
And laid her on the cement. They cut away her jeans.

Sterling and I fought all the time,
Driving around in his rotten green mustang.
I was the sweetest sixteen,
And when we hit the other car
Darkness met me at the windshield.

My father kept Sterling from the room.
I was plastered and sutured and puffed up.

When I go to heaven,
I'll think of Sterling.
I'll think that I loved him.
I'll think that he was human.
That he was a poor little brain in a dangerous body.

Side B: "Tom"

6. This Charming Man

It's gruesome that someone so handsome should care

Age twelve,
On my bicycle,
I'd fly over the bike bridge to the school.
My retainer flew from my mouth,
And I let it lie on the side of the road.

My buckteeth fling themselves from my mouth,
My ears shoot from my head like handles
And my nose is a blob.

Age fifteen,
In the back of her car,
I tried it, just because.
Because boys get with girls, right?
Even ones like Medusa.

Age sixteen,
I find that I have the love life of the octopus,
Groping and grappling,
And after, slink sideways back to my home.

I would go out tonight,
But I think I'll pass.
Just because.

Age fourteen, fifteen, sixteen, and seventeen,
Erica was with Sterling
All those years,
And I was on the sideline.

We all grow older.
But they won't.
Erica won't and Sterling won't.
Sterling, please.

At home,
Nineteen-ninety-three,
There are songs on my stereo that tell me big things,
And I have a religion about myself.

Kurt Cobain tells me
Where I'm going.
Sterling, there is *this* life
And there are after lives,
And I'll see you in one of those.

7. Reel Around the Fountain

People see no worth in you
Oh, but I do.

In the parking lot,
In the 'stang,
After school,
Before his practice,
They kissed, hard.

Lips to lips,
Sharp teeth to sheep teeth.
A ritual.

Every day, from then on,
I would watch
From across the lot,
One practice,

Then another.
I'd sit at the top of the bleachers,
Trying to sink into the wood.
Watching Speedos and listening to faggot jokes.

I have dreams of water.
I have dreams of fire.
I dream of blood.
I am all of these things.

I will never marry.

8. Hand In Glove

We can go wherever we please
And everything depends upon
How near you stand to me

It's not like any other love
This one is different,
Because it's us.

When I see your chest crest above
The level of the pool,
It is Christ splashing through the blue
With a yellow ball
Here to save me.

And when I see you drive in your mustang
Arched behind the wheel
Ray Bands
Blond,
It's sexy Satan.

Graduation day,
I'll be gone.
And you,
You never knew me.

I'll keep a room
For you
In my mind.
There is a table, a chair
And a candle,
That burns forever.

9. William, It Was Really Nothing

This town has dragged you down.

It rains.

Sterling,
It was only your whole life.
In this town,
You were king.

How could something like Erica
Capture your attention?
You are a force
And so am I.

Can't you see that thinking is nothing?
That school is nothing?
That family is nothing?
That girls are nothing?

I have some advice for you,
I am the center of all,
I am the core,

And all the movements you ever made
Were made to fit into this poem

This poem that I wrote.
You are mine.

10. How Soon is Now?

I go about things the wrong way

I am my father's son
Shy and vulgar,
And the heir of shit.

You say I do it all wrong.

I fill my days
With videogames of love
And television shows;

Nineteen-ninety-five
Was a bad year.
You were everything
And,

I wiped you clean
With alcohol.

Now
I stand alone.

Something is going to happen.
Things will change.

I've erased the past,
I'm ready for the future.
For a future of me,
Without the need of you.

It's gonna happen
Now.

But when?

Thanks for reading

If you enjoyed this volume—and even if you didn't—please consider posting a review on Amazon.com to help others discover new writers. To inquire about authors or advertising, or to submit work for consideration, please contact us at:

113crickets@dymaxicon.com

We would like to thank Dymaxicon's parent company, Agile Learning Labs, and our community of patrons (shown on the following pages) for their confidence in our mission, and for their kind support in helping us meet our publication costs for this issue.

No PowerPoint bullets.

No magic bullets.

Just happier teams building better software and delivering more value, faster.

www.AgileLearningLabs.com

713 Broadway East : Seattle, WA : 98102
AdasBooks.com

SAN FRANCISCO WRITERS CONFERENCE
A CELEBRATION OF CRAFT, COMMERCE & COMMUNITY

*Find your genre here... and quite possibly
the agent and publisher you need, too!*

2012 San Francisco Writing for Change Conference
Sept. 15th, Unitarian Universalist Center

2013 San Francisco Writers Conference
Feb. 14-18, The Mark Hopkins - all genres!

Learn more at SFWriters.org

Hot People. Hot Coffee.
www.RistrettoRoasters.com

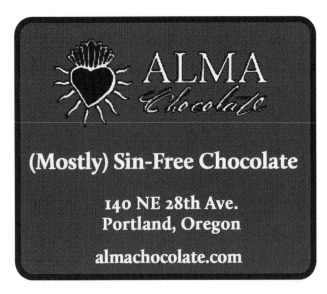

(Mostly) Sin-Free Chocolate

**140 NE 28th Ave.
Portland, Oregon**

almachocolate.com

If you like what you've read in this and other editions of 113 Crickets, you may enjoy these titles from Dymaxicon, all of which are available for purchase on Amazon.com.

DYMAXICON

DYNAMIC + MAXIMUM + CONTENT

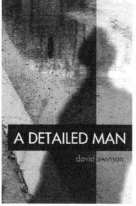

A DETAILED MAN
David Swinson

A relentless tour of DCs most crime-ridden streets, with many beautifully written surprises, and darker than the deepest noir.

Madison Smartt Bell

David Swinson captures perfectly the jaded attitude of a veteran cop in the big city.

Alan Lengel

SHORT FUSE
Lili Ristagno

Like sorting through postcards sent from a godless middle America-or leafing through a madman's high school yearbook.

John Chandler
Portland Monthly

A mass-murdering couple. So romantic! And no one could have captured this particular infamous couple like Ms. Ristagno has. Beautiful art and storytelling!

Peter Bagge

WWW.DYMAXICON.COM

DYMAXICON

DYNAMIC + MAXIMUM + CONTENT

PHYSICAL CULTURE
Hillary Louise Johnson

The single most shattering novel I've read since Jerzy Kosinski's The Painted Bird.

Harry Crews

Hillary Johnson has achieved in Physical Culture a sort of perfect, corrupt beauty.

Patrick McGrath

THE BAD MOTHER
Nancy Rommelmann

Utterly harrowing and sweet, alien and recognizable all at the same time.

Erica Schickel

You may find it hard to look at these beautifully desperate characters, but it's much harder to look away.

David Rensin

Made in the USA
Charleston, SC
27 July 2012